Against This

Maxwell Bodenheim

Alpha Editions

This Edition Published in 2021

ISBN: 9789354846090

Design and Setting By
Alpha Editions
www.alphaedis.com
Email – info@alphaedis.com

As per information held with us this book is in Public Domain. This book is a reproduction of an important historical work. Alpha Editions uses the best technology to reproduce historical work in the same manner it was first published to preserve its original nature. Any marks or number seen are left intentionally to preserve its true form.

TABLE OF CONTENTS

BABY	- 1 -
NIGHTMARE AND SOMETHING DELICATE	- 3 -
REGARDING AN AMERICAN VILLAGE	- 15 -
THREE PORTRAITS	- 19 -
DEFINITIONS	- 22 -
TO A CORPULENT SINGER	- 24 -
TOPSY-TURVY	- 26 -
REVILE THE ACROBAT	- 28 -
COMPULSORY TASKS	- 30 -
RHYMED CONVERSATION WITH MONEY	- 33 -
HIGHLY DELIBERATE POEM	- 36 -
POEM	- 38 -
REALISTIC CREATOR	- 39 -
CITY STREETS	- 40 -
DECADENT CRY[A]	- 41 -
GIRL	- 43 -
COLOR AND A WOMAN	- 45 -
RELUCTANT LADY	- 47 -

PSYCHOLOGY FROM MARS	- 48 -
TO TIME	- 51 -
DECADENT DUET	- 53 -
POEM TO A POLICEMAN	- 56 -
INTIMATE SCENE	- 58 -
NEW YORK CITY	- 61 -
WE WANT LYRICS	- 63 -
A VISITOR FROM MARS SMILES	- 66 -
SURPRISE	- 68 -

BABY

1

The blue beginning of your eyes
Condenses the sprawling and assured
Blue with which the sky retreats
From those obscene confessions known as days.

2

Again, your battling mites of blue
Try to stop the revolving monster of life
And find the indelible persuasiveness
Of single forms within the circling blur.
Sundered bits of a soul
Astonished at their shrunken estate,
They are not sure that they have still survived,
And plead for the conviction of sight.

3

But when they recollect
The hugely placid manners
Of their life, before the earthly exile
Made them small and fastened
To one pathetic puzzle,
Their blue reverts to swelling reveries
Whose outward circles spurn the curtained jail.

4

Upon your softly incomplete

Face, where germs of devils stir in curves

That tremble into questioning symmetries,

A thrust of darkness sometimes interferes

With secret, virgin places underneath

Your eyes and where your leaf-thin nostrils pause.

This darkness bends with helpless messages,

Like history admonishing a world

Personified in one, composite face.

NIGHTMARE AND SOMETHING DELICATE

You mutter, with your face

Pleading for more room because

It has scanned a panorama:

You mutter, with every difference

On your face an error in size

Mesmerized by the sight of a sky-line:

"Life is a nightmare and something delicate."

Lady, they have made a world for you,

And if you dare to leave it

They will flagellate you

With the bones of dead men's thoughts,

And five senses, five termagants

Snapping at the uneasy mind.

"No, five riotous flirts,"

You say, "and each one has

A thick blandishment to master the mind."

Yes, lady, through the bold disarrangement of words

Life acquires with great foresight

An interesting nervousness.

But O lady with a decadent music

Somehow silent in lines of flesh,

Finding your face too small,

Finding the earth too small,

Have they not informed you

That crowding life into seven words

Is an insincere and minor epigram?

And have they not reprimanded you

Because you fail to observe

Their vile and fervent spontaneity,

These howlers of earthly shrouds?

And have they neglected to drive

The bluster of their knuckles against your face

Because you rush from the leg and arm

Anecdotes of microscopical towns,

Bandying with a fantasy

Which they call thin and valueless?

"Life is a nightmare and something delicate,"

You repeat, and then, "O yes, they have done these things

To me because I take not seriously

The interval between two steps

Made by Death, who has grown a little tired.

When Death recovers his vigor

The intervals will become

Shorter and shorter until

No more men are alive.

But now they have their chance.

The wild, foul fight of life

Delights in refreshing phrases—

Swift-pouring tranquillities and ecstasies

Atoning for the groaning stampede

That desecrates the light

Between each dawn and twilight.

And those who stand apart

Use the edged art of their minds

To cut the struggling pack of bodies

Into naked, soiled distinctness."

Lady, do not let them hear you.

You are too delicate—

Deliberately, nimbly, remotely, strongly

Delicate—and you will remind them

Too much of Death, who is also

The swiftly fantastic compression

Of every adjective and adverb

Marching to nouns that live

Beyond the intentions of men.

Men are not able, lady,

To strike his face, and in vengeance

They will smear your face

With the loose, long hatred of their words.

I will wash your face

With new metaphors and similes,

Telling carefully with my hands

That I love you not for your skin,

And every bird at twilight

Will be enviously astonished

At your face now insubstantial

Indeed, you have an irony

That ironically doubts

Whether its power is supreme,

And at such times you accept

The adequate distraction

Of cold and shifting fantasy.

This is your mood and mine,

And with it we open the window

To look upon the night.

The night, with distinguished coherence,

Is saying yes to the soul

And mending its velvet integrity

Torn by one forlorn

Animal that bounds

From towns and villages.

The night is Blake in combat

With an extraordinary wolf

Whose head can take the mobile

Protection of a smile;

Whose heart contains the ferocious

Lies of ice and fire;

Whose heart with stiff and sinuous

Promises swindles the lips and limbs of men;

Whose heart persuades its confusion

To welcome the martyred certainties

Of cruelty and kindness;
Whose brain is but a calmness
Where the falsehoods of earth
Can fashion masks of ideas.
Welcome the wolf.
Bring lyrics to fondle his hair.
Summon your troops of words
And exalt his gasping contortions.
Lady, it is my fear
That makes me give you these commands.
Men will force upon you
The garland of their spit
If you fail to glorify,
Or eagerly disrobe,
The overbearing motives of their flesh.
And every irony of yours
Will be despised unless
A hand of specious warmth
Directs the twist of your blades.
O lady, you are flashing detachment
Clad in exquisitely careful
Fantasy, and on your face
Pity and irony unite
To form the nimble light of contemplations.
Men will dread you as they fear
Death, the Ultimate Preciosity.

Stay with me within this chamber

And tell me that your heart

Is near to a spiral of pain

Curving perfectly

From the squirming of a world.

See, you have made me luminous

With this news, and my heart,

Fighting to be original,

Ends its struggle in yours.

Turning, we trace a crescent

Of conscious imagination

Upon the darkness of this room.

Night and window still remain.

Night, spiritual acrobat,

Evades with great undulations

The moans and exultations of men.

His madly elastic invitation

To the souls of men

Gathers up the imagination

Of one poet, starving in a room

Where rats and scandals ravish the light.

With conscious combinations of words

The poet bounds through space with Night.

Together they observe

The bleeding, cheated mob

Of bodies robbed by one quick thrill.

Cold, exact, and fanciful,

They drop the new designs of words

Upon a vastly obvious contortion.

Poet and night can see

No difference between

The peasant, groveling and marred,

And smoother men who cringe more secretly.

Yet they give these men

The imaginary distinctions of words.

Compassionate poet and night.

You say: "With glaring details

Attended by the voices of men,

Morning will attack the poet.

Men will brandish adjectives.

Tenuous! Stilted! Artificial!

Dreams of warm permanence

Will grasp the little weapons

Furnished by the servant-mind.

Dreams … ah, lady, let us leave

The more precise and polished dream

Of our sadness, and surpass

The scoundrel, beggar, fool, and braggart

Fused into a loose convulsion

Called by men amusement.

Laughter is the explosive trouble

Of a soul that shakes the flesh.

Misunderstanding the signal
Men fly to an easy delight.
Causes, obscure and oppressed,
Cleave the flesh and become
Raped by earthly intentions.
Thus the surface rôles of men
Throw themselves upon the stranger,
Changing his cries with theirs.
The aftermath is a smile
Relishing the past occurrence.
Lady, since you desire
To clutch the meaning of this sound and pause,
Laugh and smile with me more sadly
And with that attenuated, cold
Courage never common to men.
Another window is behind us,
Needing much our laugh and smile.

II

That metaphysical prank
Known as chance—overwhelming
Lack of respect for bodies
And the position of objects—
Gathers three men and arranges them
Side by side in a street-car.
Freudian, poet, and priest—
Ah, lady, they have not lost

The unreal snobbishness
With which their different minds
Withdraw from one another.
Their thought does not desire
Only to be distinct
And adventurous.
They must also maintain
An extreme aloofness;
Throw the obliterating adjective;
Fix a rock and perch upon it.
Chance, the irresistible humorist,
Has lured their bodies together,
With that purity of intention
Not appreciated by men.
With a smile not impersonal
But trampling on small disputes,
We scan the minds and hearts of these men.
The Freudian is meditating
Upon a page within his essay
Where the narrative sleep of a woman
Clarifies her limbs and breast.
He does not know that men
Within their sleep discover
Creative lips and eyes stamped out by life;
That coarse and drooling fish-peddlers
Change to Dostoyevskies;

Morbid morgue-attendants
Snatch the sight of Baudelaire;
Snarling, cloudy cut-throats
Steal the shape of François Villon.
Men within their slumber
Congratulate the poetry,
Prose, and art that life reviles
Within their stifled consciousness.
Their helpless imaginations
Throw off the soiled and cramped
Weight of memorized realities.
The Freudian in the street-car
Ties this freedom to a creed,
Narrowing the broad escape
Until it fits the lunge of limbs.
We leave him, rubbing his nose
To catch the upheaval of triumph,
And look upon the more removed
Body of the poet.
Lady, poets heal
Their slashed and poisoned loneliness
With words that captivate
The bald, surrounding scene:
Words that grip the variations
Crowded underneath each outward form,
Governed by the scrutiny

Of mind, and heart, and soul.

Transcending the rattle of this car

And every other gibberish

Uttered by civilization,

The poet plans his story.

Life, an old man, cryptic and evanescent,

Tries to sell some flowers

To Death, who is young and smiles.

Lady, this poet is also young—

Tingling, candid somersault of youth—

And his words only catch

Surface novelties of style.

Different phrases drape one thought.

"An old man 3 thirds asleep"

Replaces "an old man completely asleep."

Ah, these endless dressmakers.

They hang a new or faded gown

Upon the shapes of life:

They do not cut beneath the mould

And clutch the huddled forms that wait

For resurrection in the inner dungeon …

Poet and Freudian leave their seats

To gain the sleek encouragement of supper,

And only the priest remains.

From the lumbering torture of years

Men have wrenched a double hope,

God and Christ, and sought to calm

The strained deceptions of their flesh.

Lady, the tarrying soul,

Patient and flexible,

Must often smile at the simple,

Crude anticipations of men.

This priest smiles and is sleepy,

Thinking of coffee with cognac,

And the warm, assuring duty of prayer.

The outer smile is ever

An unconscious obliteration.

Ah, lady, logics, masks,

And ecstasies forever

Spurn the pregnant, black

Mystery that lets them spend

The tense importance of a moment.

Only fantasy and irony,

Incongruous brothers,

Can lift themselves above

The harassed interval that Death permits.

REGARDING AN AMERICAN VILLAGE

I

O local mannerisms,

Coarsely woven cloaks

Thrown upon the plodding,

Emaciated days within this village,

I have no contempt or praise

To give you—no desire

To rip you off, discovering

Skin, and undulations known as sin,

And no desire to revise you

With glamorous endearments of rhyme.

Slowly purchased garments

Of cowardice, men wear you

And aid their practised shrinking

From one faint irritation

Escaping nightly from their souls.

Night makes men uncertain—

The mystery of a curtain

Different from those that hang in windows.

At night the confidence of flesh

Becomes less strong and men

Are forced to rescue it

With desperate hilarities.

Observe them now within the bland
Refuge of manufactured light.
Between the counters of a village store
They arm their flesh with feigned
Convictions brought by laughter.
Afterwards, as they roll along
The dark roads leading to their farms,
The grumbling of their souls will compete
With the neighing of horses
And the stir of leaves and weeds.
Night will lean upon them,
Teasing the sturdiness of flesh.

II

The body of Jacob Higgins—
Belated minstrel—sings and dances
On the edge of the cliff.
Once fiendish and accurate,
His greed has now become
Frivolous and unskillful,
Visualizing Death as a new
Mistress who must be received with lighter manners.
Preparing for her coming
He buys "five cents wuth of candy"
For a grandchild, and with a generous cackle
Tackles a chair beside the stove.
Another old man, like a blurred

Report of winter, seizes
The firmer meaning of a joke
About the Ree-publican partee.
Jacob, using one high laugh,
Preens himself for celestial dallying.
Old men in American villages laugh
To groom the mean, untidy habits
Of their past existences.
(They lack the stolid frankness
Of European peasants.)

Behind a wire lattice
Bob Wentworth separates the mail
With the guise of one intent
On guessing the contents of a novel.
Forty years have massed
Exhausted lies within him,
And to ease the weight he builds
Mysteries and fictions
In the fifty people whom he knows.
Agnes Holliday receives her letter
With that erect, affected
Indifference employed by village girls.
The words of a distant lover
Rouse the shallow somnambulist
Of her heart, and it stares
Reproachfully at an empty bed.

Oh, she had forgotten:
Sugar, corn, and loaves of bread.
The famished alertness of her reading
Curtsies to a cheap and orderly
Trance known to her mind as life.
Then an anxious, skittish youth
Behind the counter invites her
To the weekly dance at Parkertown.
Concrete pleasures drive their boots
Against the puny, fruitless dream …
And, Thomas Ainsley, they have given you
Chained tricks for your legs and arms,
And peevish lulls that play with women's feet.
You stroke the paper of your letter—
An incantation to the absent figure.

The night upon a country-road
Is waiting to pounce upon
The narrow games of these people.
The power of incomprehensible sounds
Will cleave their breasts and join
The smothered gossip of trees,
And every man will lengthen his steps
And crave the narcotic safety of home.
Fear is only the frantic
Annoyance of a soul,
Misinterpreted by flesh.

THREE PORTRAITS

I

Withdraw your hair from the simulated
Interest of the moon;
Take every tenuous shadow
From the aimless tongues of these trees
And darken your speech until it attains
A fickle and fantastic
Acquaintance with the eccentric night;
Disarrange your dress and make it
A subtle invitation to nakedness.
Remove your shoes and stockings
So that your feet may enjoy
An embarrassed soliloquy with the grass;
Place the palm of your hand
Lightly against your nose,
Following the slope of some grotesque feeling.
Devise these careful affronts
To the heavier intentions
Of thought and emotion, and gratefully
Accept your title of minor poet.

Only trees with long roots caught by hills
Will recognize your importance.

II

They worship musical sound,
Protecting the breast of emotion.
Their feelings pose as fortune-tellers
And angle for coins from credulous thoughts.
Shall we abandon this luxury
Of mild mist and wild raptures?
Your face refrains from speaking yes
But your poised eyes roundly
Reward the luminous question.
Greece and Asia have exchanged
Problems upon your face,
And the fine poise of your head
Tries to catch their conversation.
Few people care to use
Thought as a musical instrument,
Bringing ingenious restraints to grief and joy,
But we, with clasped arms, will descend
Daringly upon this situation.
The full-blown confusion of life
Will detest our intrusion.

III

If you subtract a nose you add religion,
Supine, and in a glitter of explanation

Expanding the unreasonable second
Of chattering, pugnacious flesh.
The inquisitive elevation of noses
Does not fit into the smooth
Curvatures of faith.
If you remove the lips you add
Philosophy, for lips express the warm
Quarrel of emotions and become
Crimson antagonists to contemplation.
If you subtract the eyes you add
The fertile smugness of earth,
For eyes are rapid skeptics
Tossing light beyond the circles of earth.
Flesh will remain and vacillate
Between the cocaine of belief
And times of wakefulness
Designed to replenish the drug.
Then reconstruct the face
With shifting experiments
Of spirit, fantasy, and intellect,
Intent upon violating
The tyrannies of formal reiteration.
Men will revile you and bestow
The necessary background.

DEFINITIONS

Music is a treacherous sound,
Seducing emotions and marking
Their breathless faces with death.
Art is an intrepid mountebank,
Enraging philosophies and creeds
By stepping into the black space beyond them.
Religions are blindly tortured eyes,
Paralyzing the speed of imagination
With static postures of hope.
History is an accidental madness,
Using nations and races
To simulate a cruel sanity.
(In the final dust
This trick will be discovered.)
Psychology is a rubber-stamp
Pressed upon a slippery, dodging ghost,
But thousands of centuries can remove
All marks of this indignity.

Men, each snuggling proudly
Into an inch of plausible falsehood,
Will hate the careless smile
That whitens these definitions.
The table has been broken by fists;

The fanatic has mangled his voice;
The scientist cautiously repairs the room
Beyond which he dares not peer.
Life, they will never cease to explain you.

TO A CORPULENT SINGER

I

Bulging maturity
Constructs an unfair version
Of curves not visible
To eyes upon the outside face.

II

If a soul is more
Slender than the motives of wind,
Flesh provides the necessary
Privacy, and in a rising voice
The soul proclaims its gratefulness.

III

Who has watched a bear
Pawing his idea of a breeze?
The audience in this falsely walled
Room is pouncing awkwardly
Upon the small part of a singer's voice.
The actual sounds swing easily
To eyes and ears beyond the edge of earth.

IV

And if to this meandering
Of metaphysical remarks

I should add a face

Where tragedy experiments with lanterns

To aid a long, sharp nose and wondering lips,

And laughter is conscious of being

The excited, misunderstood child of a soul,

The singer would receive

Final details of her disguise.

TOPSY-TURVY

I

If I insist that violets
Are intellectual eyes
Dotting with a wave of sight
The chained recalcitrance of earth,
Philosophers and scientists—
Blind boys who bolt themselves within a room—
Will seek to torture me
For the flashing witchcraft
That rides on thunderclaps
Called imagination.
The crystallized escape
Of fear is known as logic,
And men have used it to light
Small spaces in the wilderness of black.
But I prefer to mount
Huge horses of the wind,
Whose fantastic laughter
Separates to metaphors
And similes that hurl their decorations
Against the wide malevolence of space.
When I return to the morbid
Helplessness of earth

And shake off the dream of freedom,
Men ply their knives of gods
And creeds upon my skin.
Much traveling through space
Has made me immune to pain,
And metaphors and similes
Aid my counting of blood-drops,
Bringing color to mathematics.

II

Lady upon whose head
I weave the motives of this poem,
Change your sex to a barely visible
Trembling that can match the fluttering charm
Of the wreath that I have made for you.
When this task is finished
We may saunter gayly
Past the cunning niches
That psychology has made for us.

REVILE THE ACROBAT

Maiden, where are you going,
With impudence that makes your arms and legs
Unnecessary feathers?
Your eyes have interceded
Between the flesh and soul,
And show a light of reconciliation.
For whom have you prepared yourself?

I go to see an acrobat
Reviled by men, and acting
Within a lonely circus owned
By Mind, Soul, & Heart, Incorporated.
I love his limbs whose muscles
Compete with twirls of gossamer,
And Oh, I love him not
With the drooling, fevered weight of earth.
He turns my blood to one
Profusion of melted wings.

Maiden, why is this acrobat
Better than men who stand within
The favored halls of mind and heart,
Playing, with lust and dignity,
Violins and trumpets?

They are not better, and he,

Whose thoughtful quickness combines

The pliantness of mind and soul,

He is not worse—the thoughts of men

Stand still on high roofs of the mind,

Or borrow sorceries of flesh,

While he, with flimsy trails

Of ruffles on a gaudy jacket,

Springs into the air; assaults

Every stately, fierce, robust

Finality that men have made.

He cares not whether he is right or wrong.

He seeks a decorative speed

Of thought and soul, and he is not afraid

Of being insincere.

Men loathe him, but I clothe him

With magnificent, specific

Fabrics slighter than the remorse of a child

And bearing involved births of colors.

Strength is not alone

The size and thickness known to men!

COMPULSORY TASKS

Words, it is apparent

That you are crucified and fondled

By the pride of each new generation.

O words, whose sportive formations

Could make the courts of intellect

Belligerent and insane,

Men have sentenced you

To scores of endless drudgeries.

Weakened by the years,

You guard the dying bonfires

Of each nation and race.

Again, like hordes of cattle,

You drag the expectations

Of social theories and remedies,

Stopping only when the blood of men

Washes away your useless labours.

I have seen your bands

Of ragged courtesans

Marching in feverish lines

To rescue the rites of sex.

I have watched you rush

To repair the cracks

In breaking cathedrals and churches.

With gilded, exclamatory vowels

You garnish the cowering of earth,

And with recurring darkness

You spurn the peering mind.

Again you are hands of intellect,

Disrobing the flesh of men

And carefully preserving

Each discarded garment

With a pinch of powdered emotion.

Again you are driven forth

In lying mobs of sighs and laughs

To warm the evening hours of a nation.

("They could never restrain themselves

To wait at home for the postman ...

Would Copperfield marry Dora or Agnes?")

Sentimental breathlessness

Fleeing from the helpless decay of thought.

O words, brow-beaten bricklayers

Obeying the shouts of science

And raising walls upon whose top

The soul is perched, contemptuously

Squinting down at toiling pygmies:

O words, and you can be

Superbly demented skeptics,

Betraying the unctuous failures of earth;

Riding the wild horse of the mind:

Bringing spurs into play;

Summoning with pain the lurking soul.

RHYMED CONVERSATION WITH MONEY

How many planets have you raped,

Where only animals escaped

To scrape with melancholy needs

The bones of last men lost in weeds?

Since you are blunt and fraudulent

You must receive a bare treatment.

Adverbs and adjectives undress

When greeted by excrescences.

You are the stench on any street,

Thick with the vagaries of defeat:

The wench who plies her squawking crime

Within the alley-ways of time.

For men desire to guard with pain

The limitations of their brain,

And drag the numbness of their hearts

Within ornate and creaking carts.

And for these tasks they must be bold,

Clutching endurance from a cold

Squirming with you within the dark,

And rising blistered with your mark.

Again you give to doubting lust

An argument which it can trust.

Imagination spoils the scene

And needs a dagger, crude and mean.

For you were made by men to choke

A lyric with an obscene joke

And strike the mind when it is strong,

With whips methodical and long.

Men who are inarticulate

Desire to parody their fate

With gibberish of clinking coins.

When life, excited thief, purloins

The voice and energy of men,

They lead him to a mouldy pen:

They seek revenge and watch him wilt,

Finding importance in his guilt.

They do not know that they have made

The thief to revel in his aid.

And you are there to strain your cheek

Against imaginations weak—

Coquettish counterfeit of strength.

I have observed your metal length

Of hands drop on the poet's throat,

And yet he scarcely saw you gloat.

To certain men you merely feed

The stoics of creative need.

Money

I am the vicious test with which

Men find that they are poor or rich.

Without my challenge men might fail

To leave the blurred and murderous jail.

Utopias are merely death:

Men need the scorching of my breath.

HIGHLY DELIBERATE POEM

"Mother o' mi-i-ine, mother o' mi-i-ine,

Sweet as uh ro-ose in thuh spring-ti-i-ime"—

The man who bawls this song

Has the face of a spell-bound, hairless rat.

Entranced within a spotlight,

He borrows unconsciously

Another voice from despair.

The ordinary squeak of his life

Is paralyzed, and fear of death

Lends him a tenor voice

To supplicate the Catcher.

But the audience fails to understand

And makes flat sounds of glee

With hands ... Death, quietly

Disgusted at this blind approval,

Takes away the spotlight.

Now safe, the rat presents

Jerks of gratitude and scampers off

To gnaw at his wife within their dressing-room.

That squeezed-in bag of piteous

Mythologies described as heart

Has opened in one thousand people

And received a vision

Of past solicitude for other bags.
The rat repeats this feat and wins
Varieties of coarse sweetmeats.
At sixty the rat will be a gorged
Machiavelli, wondering
Whether he has not blundered.
Death finds no interest in killing rats
And often allows them to live,
Preferring instead the less buried souls
Of a poet or a child of ten.
But the rat has found a fear
Within the second eyes of whiskey
And relates it to his wife.
"Say, May, this thing is funny!
You won't believe me, but tonight
Just before I started the act
I felt like I was gonna die.
What in hell is wrong with me?
This booze must be drivin' me bughouse.
Well, move a leg, and get that thousand
Faulkner promised you, and stop
Sitting there and staring at me."
Death, who has listened with fastidious
Ennui, strolls off to slay
A negro infant newly born.

POEM

A curious courtship in your brain
Regulates the movements of your limbs.
Remorse, the fanciful, abandoned
Child of madness, discovers its lips
Upon the breast of a hovering Madonna.
How many poets present
The crushed tips of their hearts
Pieced carefully together as a wreath
Upon the two heads of this wooing?
Imagination is a wound
Upon the adventures of thoughts,
And one scar left behind
Is known as reality.
Will they give you robes
Threaded with orderly shimmers of repentance,
Pardoning the scar in earthly ways?

REALISTIC CREATOR

A Sonnet Dedicated to T. S. Eliot

An intimate and playful accident
Common to life had placed him on a bench
Beside an old and stiffly wounded wench.
With erudite and careful eyes he sent
A sneer to tear away her feeble mask
And snatch the battered dullness of her heart.
He spied her only in the scheming part
Of soiled flesh bickering with some trivial task.

The lacerated madness of her soul,
And delicate emotions kicked by life,
Did not invade the swift tricks of his mind.
Regarding her, he could not see the whole,
Or catch the psychic lunge behind her strife.
His eyes were savagely adroit, and blind.

CITY STREETS

This pavement and the sordid boast of stone
And brick that wins the pity of a sky
Are only martyred symbols made to buy
A dream of permanence for flesh and bone.
The jumbled, furtive anecdotes of lips
And limbs that bring their fever to this street,
They will subside to fragments of defeat
Within the cool republic where death trips.

This is an age where flesh desires to shape
Intense hyperboles in prose and verse,
Transforming city streets and country lanes
To backgrounds aiding physical escape.
But city streets are waiting to disperse
With ruins the fight and plight of earthly pains.

DECADENT CRY[A]

Hill-flowers salute his feet

Upon the upward slant of a path.

His destination does not matter.

His legs divide the spacious tragedy

Of distance into the small translation

Of steps, and with their aid he reaches

The fraudulent temple of a pause or end.

Hill-flowers, important and unprejudiced,

Bow to this monster-clown.

His feet, ridiculous and neat,

Do not stop, for they must ape

A certainty and hasten to attack

Or praise fixed idols made by flesh and mind.

Hill-flowers, trimly polished

Devices hailing preciosity;

Rumpled by the wind

To scores of original caprices;

Bearing the transfigured skirmish

Of spiritual moods that men call color;

Swiftly and unassumingly

Deaf to lusts and traditions—

They are not regarded

By the men who walk, flat-footed,

Or with scholarly exactitude,

In chase of an ardent chicanery

Known as flesh, and elderly

Quibbles of mind and emotion.

Only an intellect clad in sprightly chiffon

Can spy the importance of flowers on a hill.

> [A] *Dedicated to a rare moment of intelligence on the part of The Dial.*

GIRL

The words of men are not conjectures
Lunging toward your soul:
They do not wish you to leave
The fawning thefts of flesh.
When with covered formality
They tramp from actual pulpits,
They merely bring celestial nonsense
For one, uncurious, sanctified bed.
Ah, girl, the soul that they give you
Is a clumsy, white
Concert-master rebuking
The first-violin of your body.
Again they brand a word,
Sacredness, upon your breast,
Claiming that your soul is tied
To the pliant riot of your limbs.

Girl, I can forget for a moment
That hairs upon the bulge of my chest
Must be praised or censured,
And I have no desire
To belittle you with one,
Hopeless, cynical, sententious
Group of words, while intellect,

Flavoring its tea-cup with a sneer,
Watches you from shaded balconies.
When you win the torpid illness
Known as virtue you are less important
Than a quest for daisies in the moon,
And when you merely ask
For one blow and inertness,
An old dream yells and ends
With the quietness of sprawling pity.
Girl, avoid the plentiful
Drugs of seriousness and spend
Pieces of your heart on every whim.
Give your flesh the light and sharp
Contacts of a thistle blown
Across the wincing cheeks of rogues.
Make your soul and body spurn
Each other with a swift impertinence,
And let your clawing griefs and joys
Be still a moment on the couch of thought.
And if at times you turn your head
To spy the hatred of philosophers
And panting realists, preserve the smile
Of one who takes a suitable reward.

COLOR AND A WOMAN

Cry the names of colors
And fail to reproduce
The brightly worried way
In which they burn ideas,
Sweeping hues of intangible blood
Into the conspiring fires of soul:
The darkly reticent manner
With which they embalm emotions,
Ending the spontaneous treachery
With a self-possessed attraction.
Chant the names of colors
And fascinate the brown
Coward, who surrounds himself
With crystal safeguards known as facts,
But likes the dangerous sounds
Of unattained realities.
Or, scorn this satirical advice
And storm the body of a woman
With words as deliberate as wind,
Yet heavier, and bearing
Colors without a label.
The substance of her hair—
Ethereal stems that continue their quest
Beyond the warped confines of sight—

Shows the darkness of intellect

Answering a miniature sunset

Whose dying light does not quite succumb.

The steep reserve of her forehead

Has been kindled by a flat burden

Pale as the cry of a child, yet carrying

The hint of trouble found in late afternoon.

Her eyes hold emotional evening,

With spurts of dawn remaining like anxious relics

Kept alive by unsatisfied designs

From that derided realm where logic dies.

Her breast is the color that a north wind

Would have if it were visible to eyes.

Upon her body, color in light and darkness

Subdues the ribald ponderousness of life

And brings the filmy, flashing seriousness

Detested by the prostrate toil of mud;

Hated in taverns at midnight;

Banished from every couch when morning

Rearranges the ancient jest.

RELUCTANT LADY

The widely bruised, shy beauty of a brain
That renders dogmas bashful with its breath
Will raise its last, wan offering to death—
A poise of gossamer that takes the rain
Of darkness, with an unexpectant pride.
Your thoughts are old and yet too young for life
Whose ponderous sneer preserves their curling strife.
They wait for heavy spear-points, side by side.

You are a wilted pilgrim on a road
Where hills and rubbish-pits receive alike
The skeptical remonstrance of your pace.
You pass through towns and raise your thoughtful load
To shield your loves against the words that strike
The sheer, elastic trouble of your face.

PSYCHOLOGY FROM MARS

Torban flattered the details
Of his festival in brown—a beard—
With fingers that held a musical length,
And spoke of psychology.
The clever reproduction
Of a human being,
His appearance lacked
A hairsbreadth of reality
And barely failed to convince.
His eyes, assemblages of planets
Miraculously dwarfed, were small
But did not hold the shifting gluttony
Common to little eyes.
His lips were unsubstantial fibres
And the straight line of his nose
Gained an unearthly sincerity.
His body was muscular but failed to reveal
The smug delusion of superiority
That lives within physical strength.
With a voice in which pity and satire
Mingled bewilderedly with each other,
He spoke of psychology.
"Normal and average men
On Mars are charged with being

Insane and distorted oracles.
Because they desire to resemble each other
We force them to live together
On drably elaborate plateaus.
There they fashion cities—
Geometrical madness
That censures shreds of dread and unrest
Within the spaces of its heart.
There they retreat to farms,
And the disciplined exhaustion
Of their lives reclines upon
Monotonous rewards known as harvests.
They cling to homes—slumbering alcoves
Plentifully supplied
With complimenting mirrors
And altars for the mind.
Sometimes a revolution
Seduces their living flatness,
And an original confusion
Follows rumours of creation,
But the sanity vanishes
Into the marching unison
Of their repentant madness.
We who are sane live below the plateaus.
'Home' to us is a flitting answer:
Different spots inevitably

Transformed by our bodies garlanded with mind,

Or requests of the heart

That tarry a moment for shelter.

As we wander we tear

And rebuild ancient lanes and houses,

Leaving a sentinel of change

Behind to confront the next traveller.

We stroll in twos and threes

That endure for a day or an hour,

And we never linger

At one place to gloat over details.

Restless sanity, my friend,

Equips the changing cries within us.

Restless sanity

Prevents us from complacently

Dozing over miniatures,

With a dream of importance

Rocking within the rhythms of our hearts!"

TO TIME

O Time, you are an idiot's fluid curse.

O Time, you are an uninspired hearse.

O Time, you kill beneath your robe of nurse.

O Time, your eyes are cherubs drowned in pools,

O Time, your wisdom scorns the aid of stools,

O Time, your kindness blinds the life of fools.

O Time, you blur pretentious intellect.

O Time, you break the thrones that thoughts erect.

O Time, your hands indifferently correct

The incoherent sorceries of men

Who dance before a monstrous Axe and Pen,

Waving the fetiches of words, and then

Censure the dance with pedestals of gauze

Cleverly imitating rock, and laws

Whose opaque sureness broods above their cause.

When irony will cease to be obscure

To men whose eyes resent the cloudy lure

That ends their tiny clarities, with pure

And forming mists of words, then men will climb

With restless regularity, like Time,

Who merely seeks a changing pantomime.

O Time, you are too pure and swiftly wide

For men who try to check your colored stride

With opaque temples and a sleeping bride.

DECADENT DUET

Torban

Lightly sharp and even,

Your voice is the sound of an airplane

Darting high above your unreceptive face.

Your voice is unrelated

To the structure of your face,

And on your lips an echo merely rides,

The pagan shimmerings of your face

Receive the voice with a subtle disbelief.

Indeed, your intellectuality,

Speeding though spaces over your head,

Must seem of little consequence

To the nymph who listens far below.

That you are thus divided is not strange,

But you contain a third Self

And it regards the other two

With a grave and patient interest.

Woman

Phantasmagoria,

Ruling arabesques of words,

Your attenuated variations

Of thought and emotion will enrage

The blunt convictions of more earthly men.

The pagan rituals of my face

Distrust your words, and my mind,

Dropping its voice from fancied heights,

Resents the indirectness of your style.

But the third Self within me,

Generous and immobile of face,

Cares only for the skill

With which you elevate

Vainly celebrating shades

Of thought and protesting emotion.

Color, form, and substance—

Three complaining slaves

Engraving the details of prearranged tasks

Within stationary brains and hearts.

My third Self would release them

To an original abandon

That exchanges intangible countries,

With a gracious, gaudy treason.

Torban

Lacking a better name

I will call your third Self "soul."

The ancient, merry game

Of fighting over labels

Must not dismay our duet.

To most men soul exists

Only when their sensual weariness

Needs to be gilded with a religion

Or a deified memory of flesh.

We contain a lurking wanderer

Upon our inner roads, and he

Sometimes stops to drop pitying hands

Upon the forms of thought and emotions

Branded with scores of prejudices.

Men have hated him for centuries,

And hatred, symbol of sly cowardice,

Has draped its desire in false scorn

And named him Decadence.

Thus ends our decadent duet.

Come, there are roads on which we must pirouette.

The proper contrast will be furnished

By philosophers, scientists, and sensualists.

POEM TO A POLICEMAN

Marionnette-fanatic,
Your active club within this riot
Was once the passive integrity
Of a branch upon a tree.
Now without success
It tries to beat out fire
Writhing in human skulls.
The pause of nature, transformed
Survival of every memory and defeat,
Separates to bits of action
Aiding an inexplicable fever.
The hands of centuries press
These bits into another
Pause before corruption.
O pernicious circle,
I will not believe
That your parsimonious farce
Reiterates itself through space.
The souls of men achieve
An accidental dream
That seems important merely
Because the figures which it holds
Have invented small and almost
Non-existent divisions of time.

Yet, trapped within these months and years,
I turn to you, marionnette-fanatic.
You at least can bring
Diversion to my chained
Impatience as I wait for death.
How wildly you protect
The sluggish minds of men!
A calculating laziness of thought
Has created you to guard its doors,
While other men require
An outward expression of peace
Beneath which the inner struggle
Can revel in privacy.
And so, with buttons of brass
And blue uniform that lend
An incongruous dignity
To your task, you defend
The myriads of insincerities
That drape a mutilated need.
And yet, unconsciously,
And at rare times you save
The face of beauty from an old
Insult in the fists of men.
Yes, you are not entirely
Without extenuation,
Marionnette-fanatic.

INTIMATE SCENE

Bed-room, you have earned

The sympathy of dirt,

And bear upon your air

Malevolent and thwarted

Essences of men.

Many contorters of bellies

Have stirred an urgent travesty

Shielded by your greasy dusk,

And hearts have found upon your couch

A brief, delicious insult.

Cheap room within a lodging-house,

You are not merely space

For the coronation of flesh,

And your odorous bed-quilts

Need not only provoke

The casual jeering of thought.

II

Woman and her master

Close the door too quietly.

With a mien of slinking

Insecurity, the woman turns

Within the dangling darkness of the room

And mumbles orders to her man.

Anticipation and disgust
Rout each other upon her face.
Then the gas-light brings
Its feeble understanding to the room.
Woman and man slump down
Within the chairs and regard
The tired amens of their feet.
For a time weariness
Banishes the theatrical
Divisions of masculine and feminine,
But returning strength
Calls to the untrue drama.
The man demands, with practised expectation,
Money squeezed from an automatic night;
Curses at the smallness of the sum,
And cuffs his woman without intensity,
Desiring only an excuse
For the slowness of his mind.
She is not a composition
Waiting for its orchestra of pain:
His fists can merely give
An inexpensive spice
To the apathy within her.
Soon the man and woman laugh,
To kill an inner jumble of sounds
Which they cannot separate—

Nightly complaint of their souls.

He pinches one of her cheeks,

Like an Emperor deigning

To test the softness of a bauble,

And she finds within his fingers

An endurable compliment.

When morning light exposes

Each deficiency within the room,

Man and woman open their eyes.

Hallucination of fire

No longer streams over the moving screens.

Woman and her man

Stare, with disapproval, at the walls,

And their souls become

Querulous captives almost gaining lips.

Then emotional habits

Revive the earthly hoax.

Rising from the bed,

Man and woman use their voices

Reassuringly.

NEW YORK CITY

New York, it would be easy to revile
The flatly carnal beggar in your smile,
And flagellate, with a superior bliss,
The gasping routines of your avarice.
Loud men reward you with an obvious ax,
Or piteous laurel-wreath, and their attacks
And eulogies blend to a common sin.
New York, perhaps an intellectual grin
That brings its bright cohesion to the warm
Confusion of the heart, can mold your swarm
Of huge, drab blunders into smaller grace ...
With old words I shall gamble for your face.

The evening kneels between your filthy brick,
Darkly indifferent to each scheme and trick
With which your men insult and smudge their day.
When evenings metaphysically pray
Above the weakening dance of men, they find
That every eye that looks at them is blind.
And yet, New York, I say that evenings free
An insolently mystic majesty
From your parades of automatic greed.
For one dark moment all your narrow speed
Receives the fighting blackness of a soul,

And every nervous lie swings to a whole—
A pilgrim, blurred yet proud, who finds in black
An arrogance that fills his straining lack.
Between your undistinguished crates of stone
And wood, the wounded dwarfs who walked alone—
The chorus-girls, whose indiscretions hang
Between the scavengers of rouge and slang;
The women moulding painfully a fresh
Excuse for pliant treacheries of flesh;
The men who raise the tin sword of a creed,
Convinced that it can kill the lunge of greed;
The thieves whose poisoned vanity purloins
A fancied victory from ringing coins;
The staidly bloated men whose minds have sold
Their quickness to an old, metallic Scold;
The neatly cultured men whose hopes and fears
Dwell in soft prisons honored by past years;
The men whose tortured youth bends to the task
Of hardening offal to a swaggering mask—
The night, with black hands, gathers each mistake
And strokes a mystic challenge from each ache.
The night, New York, sardonic and alert,
Offers a soul to your reluctant dirt.

WE WANT LYRICS

Thousands of faces break

To one word called dramatic:

Thousands of faces attain

An over-worked, realistic

Clash of stupidities.

At first the mob spreads out

Its animated fights of lines—

Butcher with a face one degree

Removed from the dead flesh which he cuts;

Socialist whose face rebukes

The cry for justice tumbling from his lips;

Five professors of English

Whose faces are essentially

School-boys coerced by erudition;

Bank-clerk with a face

Where curiosity

Weakly contends against

The shrewd frown brought by counting slips of money;

Girls whose first twenty years

Have merely shown them the exact

Shade of pouting necessary

For the gain of price-marked objects;

Boys with cocksure faces

Where an awkward lyric

Wins the vitriol of civilization;

Shop-girl whose face is like

The faint beginning of a courtezan

Prisoned by the trance of unsought labor;

Wealthy man whose face

Holds a courteous, bored

Reply to traces of imagination;

Housewife with a round

Face where dying disappointments

Flirt with hosts of angel-lies;

Old men with faces where a psychic doubt

Invades the ruins of noses, lips, and eyes

And dreams of better structures;

Old woman with a face

Like a bashful rag-picker

Rescuing bits of cast-off deviltries

Beneath the ebbing light of eyes.

Stare upon these faces,

With emotion cooled by every

Bantering of thought,

And they fade to one disorganized

Defeat that craves the smooth

Lubrications of music.

The mob upon this street

Reiterates one shout:

"We want lyrics! Give us lyrics!"

Space, and stars, and conscious thought

Stand above the house-tops of this street;

Look down with frowning interest;

Regard the implacable enemy.

A VISITOR FROM MARS SMILES

"Erudite and burnished poets seek
Pliant strength from Latin, French, and Greek
Phrases, finding English incomplete.
Or do they conceal their real defeat,
Like some juggler, faltering, who drops
Circling, rapid balls of words and stops
To relate obscure, pretentious tales,
Hiding nervous moments where he fails?"
Torban, visiting from Mars, became
Silent, and his smile, like mental fame,
Rescued the obscurity of flesh.
Then I answered with a careful, fresh
Purchase from the scorned shop of my mind.
"Men must advertise the things they find.
Erudition, tired after work,
Flirts with plotting vanities that lurk
Poutingly upon the edge of thought.
Languages and legends men have caught
Practice an irrelevant parade
With emotions morbidly arrayed."
Torban gave the blunt wealth of his smile.
"We, in Mars, have but one tongue whose guile
Does not yield to little, vain designs.
Feelings are fermented thoughts whose wines

Bring an aimless fierceness to the mind.
And a row of eyes, convinced and blind,
But we sip them carefully, for we
Do not like your spontaneity.
Children babbling on the rocks in Mars,
Shrieking as they dart in tinseled cars,
Are spontaneous, but as they grow,
We remove this noisy curse and throw
Nimbleness to rule their tongues and ears—
Juggling games that slay their shouts and fears.
Novelty to you is almost crime:
We decorate the treachery of time!"

SURPRISE

He knew that he was dead because his fingers had forgotten the art of touching and were trying to regain their ability. They were no longer able to separate different textures and surfaces, and everything held to them a preposterous smoothness that suggested an urbane, impenetrable sophistry. With a methodical despair they gripped one object after another, disputing the integrity of their condition, and when at last they capitulated he accepted the verity of his death. So far he had not sought to use his eyes or ears—he had existed only as a limited intensity of thought and emotion that directed his hands in a fight for variations in feeling. Now he discovered his sight, and in that moment avalanches of metaphors and similes—the detailed disguises and comparisons with which two eyes arbitrarily brand a comforting distinctness upon a mystery—rushed from his head and arranged themselves to form a world. This was a reversal of life, since in life the human eye detects and reflects the objects around it, as all good scientists will testify, and does not first project these objects and afterwards reflect them. But this man, being dead, found that his eyes had thrown myriads of determinations upon a shapeless mass and changed it to an equal number of still and animated forms. The desires within his eyes were continually altering the objects around them, so that a tree became shifting plausibilities of design and a red rose was merely an obedient chameleon. Of course, this could never have happened in life, since in life different shapes hold a fixed contour, appearance, and meaning, but this man was fortunate enough to be dead, so his eyes meddled incorrigibly with the shapes and colors which they imagined that they had made.

He sat in a room constructed by himself, and after he had become conscious of the result he saw that it was a hotel-room located in Detroit, Michigan. He examined the furniture, walls, and floor, and they were to him the firmness of his imagination divided into forms that sheltered the different needs within him. If he had still been alive he would have accepted the reality of shapes made by the majority-imaginations of other men, regardless of whether they pleased him or not, but death had given him a more audacious vigor and the room in which he was sitting did not resemble to his eyes the same chamber in which he had once reclined during his living hours. He knew that the power of his desire had returned him to a hotel-room in Detroit, Michigan, and had disarranged everything except its location and exact position. The floor was an incandescent white and suggested a proudly prostrate expanse—it did not have the supine appearance that pine and oak floors hold to the eyes of life. The furniture had lost its guise of being too economically pinned down by curves and angles, and its lines were more relaxed and disordered. The chairs were comfortable without relinquishing an aesthetic sincerity of line—a semblance scarcely ever held by chairs that figure in life—and the top of the table was not flat but depressed and elevated in different places, since the imagination of this dead man had dared to become more unobstructed. The bed had an air of counseling as well as supporting, and its posters were high and curved in above the center of a gently sloping bowl that formed the bottom. Also, the walls of the room stood with a lighter erectness in place of the rooted, martinet aspect that walls present to living eyes, while the ceiling gave an impression of cloth that could be easily flung aside and had not been spread by a passion for flat concealment.

As the dead man sat in this room which he had revised, his memory began to distribute pains throughout his brain, and he realized that the room had dominated the last third of his life. The room had been the scene of his final meeting with a woman whom he loved, for a week later she had died after being thrown from a horse. Within this room they had spoken and touched for the last time on earth, and afterwards the room had become to him a square world isolated in a possibly round world—a continent in quality and not in size, where he could disrupt the imaginative lines fashioned by other men, changing a rose to an intellectual face if he so desired. Every visual detail and remembered word of the woman had merged to a guardian silence, enclosing this separate world with alert sentinels of understanding. He recollected these affirmations with the satisfaction of a transforming creator, for his experiences had become fantasies which his memory strove to make real. This was, however, the result of his death for, as all good men will tell you, the memory of living beings is entirely different and often adds inaccurate touches to the reality of experience, making this reality fantastic and untrue.

His sense of hearing revived almost simultaneously with his memory, for hearing is the foremost aid in a capture of past happenings since its productions do not fade from the mind as rapidly as those of other senses. He found that his hearing was inextricably a part of thought and signified, indeed, the fragmentary release of thought, and this alteration drove from him every vestige of disbelief in his death, for he knew that in life hearing is almost always the sense used by men to divert the fatigue of their minds (the servant of meaningless ecstasies). Then his sense of smell, changed from an unseen drug to a floating search, collided with the odor of a woman—an odor that was less smooth and more candid than the natural ones held by women who are alive. Turning his head to the left, for the first time, he saw that the woman whom he loved was seated near him. Her naked body still gave the appearance of flesh curved as it had been during her life, but it was no longer a slyly prisoned invitation to his sense of touch. It aroused within him a feeling of thinly langourous intimacy and became a visible grave into which his thoughts could sink for future resurrection. It was as though a desire, once coarse and reeking with a defeated violence, had been transmuted to a longing for less fleeting and frantic pressures, while one former thrill became more diffused and deliberately sensitive, finding a possession to which the sense of touch was incidental, and not inevitable. The hemispheres of her breasts, imperfect and firm, and the long taperings of her limbs were to him forms which he wanted to envelope carefully with earnest refinements of motion, gaining in this way a less explanatory medium for his mind, and anything resembling an invasion would have seemed to him an abruptly senseless blunder. He saw that her face was still a gathering of boyish bewilderments beneath a mass of hair that had grown more cloudy, but these expressions were hugged by a light that made them unnecessary survivals of experience. He secured the impression that death was amusing itself with the trivialities of her features, while they held a perfect comprehension of the jest without abandoning their outward shapes. At this moment he became aware of the nakedness of his own body and felt the loss of that snug assurance which his skin had once given him. In its place there was a sheath that seemed hardly more than a visual flutter.

He looked up at the woman and their smiles were adeptly synchronized. Living people are apt to smile when they have hidden too little and weep when there is nothing left to hide, but the smiles of this dead man and woman were informal exercises of candour—thought adopting more perceptible and less evasive signals.

"Have you been sitting here since your death?" he asked. "No, I've also been creating on the streets of Detroit," she said. "You manage it in this way. First you drive all of the alertness out of your senses and your mind, and everything around you becomes a vibrating, shapeless substance, a little thicker than mist and hued with a gray that is almost colorless. Then you give a moderate vigor to your senses and your mind, and the substance breaks into hosts of shapes. You have attained the perceptions of an ordinary, living person and you find that you are walking on a street. During all of this time you have held back the strength of your imagination, which is alone real, but now you release it and it shoots from you and follows the commands of your desires. An old man's whiskers change to a weedy sprouting of thought, and each hair is the dangling of a different idea. You can see the decay of an empire crowding itself into a young girl's green and mean hat, and different events emerge and group themselves to seize or obliterate the color. A woman's leg becomes a fat blasphemy and within its shaking famous jelly you can spy a saint, writhing in the effort to free himself. A young man's shoulders are two, dead, delicate thoughts caught in a bulging tomb, with their ghosts speaking through each unconscious movement of his arms. The street-pavement lives and is a hard, detached hatred, sapping the strength of those who have enslaved it.... Sometimes I've returned to this room, not to rest, for weariness springs only from that thick weakness of imagination known as flesh, but to find you here before the final emphasis of your death."

"Since I'm not accustomed to being dead I must ask questions whose answers are obvious to you," he said. "Why are living beings unable to see you? How do you avoid their jostling and the rolling devices that they have made? How can we sit in a hotel-room, which must at the same time be occupied by living beings, without seeing or hearing them? Treat me as an earthly school-boy for a moment."

"Living beings dwell in realms made by their imaginations," she said. "We do not fit into these realms and consequently we are not forms that can be detected by the senses and imaginations of people who are alive. The desires of these people have created a world of objects and substantiations which does not match our own, and so our world is an independent one placed over the world of living men. With different intensities and designs of imagination we invade a shapeless substance and give it the elaborate distinctness of our longings. This substance is inert imagination, and when we make our senses and minds blank we become a part of it. Of course, I use the word imagination because death has not yet taught me a better one. Beyond the earth there are stars and space which are not controlled and shaped by our individual imaginations, and when the feet of our imaginations become light enough to rise beyond the shapeless mass which gave birth to them, we shall discover what greater imaginations in turn gave birth to the feeble beginning which formed us. And so we shall be able to discard this word, imagination, which only represents the boundaries of our desire and its attendant senses and thoughts, and gain the words of greater explanations. But before we depart from these boundaries we must make ourselves entirely clear and untroubled, and it will be necessary for us to reconstruct the last meeting that we had during our lifetimes. This meeting troubles us with an unfulfillment of imagination, and if we do not alter it the strength of our imaginations will be hampered by a recollection of former weakness. All men and women who die must return to the most swiftly vivid scene that their imaginations were able to attain during the period known as life. In this way the scene is gradually made perfect by understanding, and the imagination, shaking off the terror of past weakness and indecision, is able to float away from the substance that created it. Because our imaginations were much stronger than the ones surrounding them, we can achieve this task immediately, while other dead people must slowly grapple for this emancipation, visiting their scene in those guises which living people call ghosts."

"You must direct me," he said. "I was never much in harmony with the imaginative semblances and rituals of most living people, and now that I am dead I can scarcely remember them."

"Make your senses heavy and tight," she said. "Reduce them to a condition that approaches a stupor—a hopeful stupor such as prevails among those living men known as mystics and priests. When you have accomplished this, make little rows of imaginative objects and force your mind to squeeze itself within them, adoring some and hating others. Then try to arouse your senses by concentrating them upon a thickly plotting form that once was flesh, while still making them retain a disturbing trace of their former coma. You remember this form—separated into hairsbreadths of worship and laceration by stunted men?"

"Your description of living imagination is perfect," he said. "It will be minutely disagreeable to follow your orders, but let us complete the task quickly."

They looked away from each other, immersed in the strain of their inner labours. The room disappeared in large pieces that receded to the background of a gray substance, and consciousness left their bodies. Her body faded out while his solidified to flesh draped by the clumsy fears of clothes. Then the gray substance slowly adopted the shapes, colours, and details of a railroad station. Once more he was a suffering and encumbered poet, standing in the battling race of people and waiting for the train that would bring her to Detroit, Michigan. He paced up and down the cement platform, erasing his thoughts with the long strokes of his limbs and obsessed only by the belief that he was walking nearer to her in this fashion, since he was weary of being over-awed by distance. Because he did not associate her qualities and thoughts with those of other people he could never convince himself that she was real unless she stood beside him and spoke, and when her body was absent she became the unreal confirmation of his desires—a dream to which he had given the plausible tricks of flesh and voice. Only the return of these two things could reassure him, for she was to him far too delicately exact and mentally unperturbed to exist actually in the sweating, dense, malaria-saturated revolutions of a world.

The train arrived and he stood near the gate. People streamed out—a regiment disbanded after a lonely and forced conflict with thought in uncomfortable seats, or with diluted chatter that fascinated their inner emptiness. They were the people whose vast insistence and blundering control of the earth made him doubt the reality of the woman whom he loved. Oh, to feel once more certain that she was human—that her incredibly tenuous aloofness could stoop to the shields of flesh! Yes, she would come now, an alien straggler passively submitting to the momentum of a regiment of people. When she failed to appear he still lingered near the gate, inventing practical reasons for her absence—the packing of baggage, a delayed toilette. The iron gates shut with a thud that was to him the boot-sound of reality against his head.

He bought a newspaper; sat down in the waiting-room; and sought to submerge his distress in the hasty and distorted versions of murders, robberies, scandals, controversies, and machinations that defiled white sheets of paper. But he could see nothing save a hazy host of men fighting against or accepting the complexly sinister fever that made them mutilate each other, and weary of this often-repeated vision he dropped the paper. His mind gathered itself to that tight and aching lunge known as emotion, and morbidly he involved her in disasters—train-wrecks, suicide, the assault of another person. He began to feel that melodrama was the only overwhelming sincerity in a tangle of crafty or poorly adjusted disguises, and his emotional activity fed eagerly upon this belief. All of the paraphernalia of fatalism rose before his eyes—the small, lit stage with its puppets; the myriads of strings extending into a frame of darkness and pulled by invisible hands; the sudden and prearranged descent of catastrophe; the laughter of an audience of gods, examining the spectacle with a mixture of sardonic and bored moments. But abruptly he felt that these were merely the devices of a self-pity that sought to raise its stature by imagining itself the victim of a sublime conspiracy. He whistled some bars of a popular song, deliberately snatching at an inane relief from the industries of his mind. Then he walked back to the gates and waited for the next train, which was about to arrive. Once more the importantly fatigued stream of people; once more her absence. He had turned away from the gate when her hand questioned his shoulder.

"And so you are real and I have not been deceived," he said.

"I am as real as you care to make me," she answered. "I was hunting for a comb in my valise when the train came in. Combs always elude me."

She mentioned the name of a hotel and they walked to it in silence, for speech to them demanded an impregnable privacy that was violated by even the swiftly passing eyes and ears of other people. When they were alone in the hotel-room he watched her remove outer garments and don a kimono, with a pleasure that coerced sensual longing into an enslaved contemplation—a fire that glowed without burning.

"When I see your flesh then you are most unreal," he said. "It becomes a last garment that you have neglected to unfasten because you wish to pretend that you belong to the earth. The cupped appeal of your breasts is the subtle lie with which something infinitely abstract evades the weight of a world. There is a surprised element attached to your legs and they never seem assured in their task of supporting your torso. And yet, when your body is beyond my actual sight your reality is still doubtful, for then I lack even the uncertain evidence of your flesh. I am helpless—I cannot mingle you with cities and men, and even country roads seem heavily unwilling to hold you."

"And is it impossible for you to accept this body as a necessary, insincere contrast to my thoughts and emotions?" she asked, with lightness. "You are tensely morbid, Max. Now I shall sit on your knee. The scene is prearranged. You must promptly clutch me, in that involved manner that has made novelists famous and blurred the integrity of poets. The earth has anointed and pointed riots waiting for you!"

His fingers studied the short brown curls on her head and his lips touched the less obvious parts of her face—her chin, the tip of her inwardly curving nose, her temples, the meeting-place of forehead and hair.

"I can see two men looking at me now," he said. "To one I am an emasculated fool who places a dainty overtone upon his weakness, and to the other I am chaining strong desires with the lies of vain and pretty gestures. Olga, the earth is bulky and profane, and dreads anything that delicately, aloofly disputes its size!"

She carefully fitted her head between his shoulder and neck.

"This listening peace that you bring me, and the softer intentions of your hands, they are more important than the lunges of men," she said. "We are spontaneous in ways whose breathlike intensity has not been corrupted by the screaming of nerves, and Oh, we must prepare ourselves for the indifference and ridicules of a coarser audience. They cannot peer into this room, yet afterwards something within the buoyant removal of our bodies tells them to punish us with poverty and little food."

He grinned, and crowded flights of defiance were on his face.

"I've been eating onions and bread for the last week," he said. "I cut the onions into various shapes, making them resemble different articles of food. With an imaginative seriousness one can almost overcome the sense of taste. Almost."

"It is only that word that keeps us here," she said. "We are almost free illusions."

She walked to the bureau and brushed her hair, for she did not want him to see an expression on her face. He guessed it and became repentantly merry.

"Sold a poem two weeks ago," he said. "The editor wrote something about 'great originality but rather tenuous' and 'this is not a spiritual age.' It isn't."

"Let me hear it," she said.

It concerned a circle of men dumped into chairs in the lobby of a cheap lodging-house—rag-dolls twitching now and then, as though an outside hand were poking them with curiosity. Then the spirit of the lodging-house, sallow and indecently shallow, sidled into the lobby, correctly aimed its tobacco at a spitoon, and gave the dolls snores to create a false appearance of life, whereupon one of them rose and cursed the invisible intruder in his sleep. The spirit of the lodging-house, frightened and angry at the appearance of a soul whose existence it had not imagined, whisked them all off to the torture of their beds. The poem had spoken to Baudelaire and Dostoyevsky but within it a stunned hatred of the world was experimenting with appropriate symbols.

"Irrelevantly, perhaps, I'm thinking of a time when I washed dishes in a lunch-room in St. Louis," she said. "I was hunting in my mind for something that could deceive the greasy monotone of defiled chinaware. Suddenly the brown and turbid dish-water became a heavy wine, spiced with the aftermaths of earthly pleasures—decay to which a spiritual release had given a liquid significance. I became obsessed by the verity of this idea, and finally, quite entranced, I raised the pan of dirty water to my lips and was about to drink it when, at that moment, the proprietor came in. He squawked 'crazee-e,' 'crazee-e,' and discharged me. I wrote an excellent poem about it, though."

"Let's see, what would they say about this," he muttered. "Neurasthenia, insanity, exalted paranoia, minor conceit, trivial pose, empty fantasy—they have so many putrid labels to hide the inner rage, damn them!"

They swayed together in the chair, like two babies in a trap, taking the small amount of room possible in the cramped abode.

"Tomorrow we'll look for work," she said. "The breath-tablets that you bought to hide the scent of onions have not been able to eradicate a last melodramatic trace of their enemy. We must move our arms to ward off such meaningless intrusions."

"With an excellent verbosity you mock the concentration of your thoughts," he said.

They closed their eyes and grew still in the chair. When at last they stirred, each one looked first at the room and then at the other person, with a gradually slain disbelief.

"We are not dead after all," he cried. "The room does not fade away!"

They sat without moving, while happiness and sadness sprang into combat within them.

Milton Keynes UK
Ingram Content Group UK Ltd.
UKHW010704280424
441876UK00003B/118